Written by **Verity Brown**

FOUR LEGS AND A "NEIGH"!

Michael Terence
Publishing

First published in paperback by
Michael Terence Publishing in 2020
www.mtp.agency

ISBN 9781913653927

Cover image
by David Christman

Interior illustrations by
Verity Brown
www.veritybrownillustration.co.uk

I dedicate this book to some of the English teachers at my school, including Mr Burbidge who taught me how to write poetry. However, I do not include the teacher that said I had probably copied my stories from a book!

Contents

THE RED
LION
THE RED LION

Those Pony Days

Happy is the pony with a bright, white forelock
trotting through the forest in the deep, green shade;
sharing the silence
with myriads of insects
buzzing and a-hovering around each glade.

Saddle and the leatherwork creaking to the movement
urging that the rider must be alert.
Hands so neatly
hold the reins weakly
making sure the pony isn't getting any hurt.

Down goes the head as the pony takes to gallop.
"Oh," cries the gal as the trees go rushing by.
Branches make a thrashing,
clods of earth go crashing,
headlong goes the duo 'gainst a crimson sky.

Splashing through the water where the stream is shallow;
dashing through the meadows where the farmer shouts.
Knee-deep in sedges,
over the hedges;
there's none can stop this pony as it frolics here-abouts.

Canter down the High Street, traffic in a frenzy,
shoppers on the pavement dashing from the show.
Bicycle knocked over,
drunks from pubs get sober;
the rider tries to bail out but is not adept to go.

Winding up its effort, tensing like a spring,
there comes a sudden flick as it bucks real hard.
Up goes the rider,
soaring like a glider,
landing in a flowerbed in some back yard.

"You naughty little pony with a bright, white forelock,
putting all those people into disarray.
I love you so dearly
and don't care really;
…let's ride again next weekend when my bruise has gone away!"

A Mare and Her Filly

Tolerate the dungeon where my owner has imprisoned us;
scrabble in the droppings to pull out strands of hay.
    My milk for filly daughter
    is dry for lack of water.
We cannot last much longer as my owner's gone away.

Skiing down some mountain with no thought at home for us;
drinking in the bars and clubs, lazing in the sun.
    Even though she is well off,
    wouldn't buy a water trough,
so now we're left to die here; bring us help, please, anyone?

My filly has gone down now with her throat so parched as mine.
If only I could crash these bars that hold us both inside;
    prison bars that I condemn,
    so wearily I push at them
but these humans make an iron that will cause our equicide.

I see a distant window where the sunlight filters through.
The postman coming morning times but doesn't know I'm here.
    I strain to make a dried-up neigh,
    he cannot hear me anyway;
my foal is gasping on the floor, her tragic end, I fear.

I nuzzle her, my tongue so dry, I cannot lick her form;
no tears are even possible, all moisture breathed away.
    Her open eyes, an anguished smile,
    laying there immobile;
I sense our lives are ebbing down that final passageway.

But what is this, a weekend too, I hear an engine near?
A shaft of light spills onto us; the barn door swings apart.
    Overriding our cruel gaoler,
    Here comes a rescue trailer
releasing me and filly in the nick of time depart.

The moral to this story and the saving of our lives
is to monitor those places where a pony may abide.
    Rugs often used to hide its ribs,
    owners spin you loads of fibs;
ignore the lock, take a view, only you decide.

The Equine Volunteer

Dedicated worker, a volunteer to boot,
    mucking out the stables, feeding from the bin.
Dust makes you cough
and the broom head's off
    and hooves are kicking stable doors and making such a din.

Baler twine on hay bale slicing through your fingers;
    pockets bulging horse cubes; halter ties your coat.
Try to catch a pony
thinking, Oh, if only
    that little beast would come to me, not run away and gloat!

Try to give a wormer and squirt it in the mouth.
    Every dose costs many pounds; retrieve it from the straw.
Fingers now with worm slime,
try again a second time.
    Down it goes into its throat and on your bleeding paw.

Brambles score a red line striping up the forearm;
    nettles making blotches aggravate the chore.
That ragwort root
just doesn't give a hoot,
    for every time you pull it up, next year there's always more!

Trudging through the meadows in a windswept rainstorm.
    Searching in the dark for a horse called "Clown".
You call with a shout,
then your torch goes out
    and the herd of drumming hooves nearly runs you down.

Gates you try to open tied with baler twine.
    Fencing never strong enough to take the rump of horse.
Wellies tread on barbed wire,
barrow has a flat tyre;
    just an ordinary workday for a volunteer, of course!

It Wasn't an Easy Decision

Even at the ripe age of twenty-one, "Poppy", being an ex-polo Pony, still seemed to have a lot of stamina in her stride. Susan had arranged to have Poppy at the end of the polo season in early September, but it wasn't until December that she had managed to find a couple of days free to collect her from the polo stables. Poppy's owner, Jill, had five other polo horses and had decided to retire Poppy and seek a new steed to replace her for the next season.

Having loaded Poppy into the trailer at the polo stables, Susan travelled the two-hour journey back to East Sussex, unloaded her and settled her down in her new stable in a deep, straw bed with an envious pony-feed welcome. Susan considered that such an experienced, safe pony was worth thousands despite her age. Yes, she was getting on in age and probably only had another five or ten years of active service but even five or ten years was worth more for a free horse than having to pay through the nose for an up-and-coming youngster. This horse was free, but a youngster could cost thousands; in the horse world, there is a correlation between an increase in price with an increase in rider's safety.

Susan ensured that Poppy had several days to settle in to her new stables and routine and even managed to put a horse rug on when the stable became quite cold; Jill had mentioned that messing about with horse rugs for polo horses was such a chore and the ponies seemed just as happy without rugs in the stables which could be shut up from the wind chill anyway.

Saturday morning arrived and Susan decided to have her first ride to show Poppy the local village and a couple of bridle paths; there would be many more days when she could go further afield, perhaps even in the horse trailer to ride the Downs or along the beach. Anyway, Larry, the local farmer's son who lived in the village, had asked to see Poppy when she was riding out. Larry didn't get on with his father who had tried to persuade him to carry on with the farm work while Larry had other interests incompatible with manure and farm machinery.

Susan quite fancied Larry who had found lodgings at the manor house owned by Tom and Jane Roberts in return for gardening and general maintenance work. Tom was, as they say, 'something in the city' so commuted every day and Jane was heavily involved in the WI and several other village clubs. Every year they would open their five acres of garden and lawns for the villagers to raise funds for local needs like the church bells or the children's recreation area.

Susan not only spent time grooming Poppy before tacking up but spent a while in front of the tack-room mirror checking her own appearance in case she should bump into Larry. Indeed, she had decided over several days to make her first hack out to go past the manor house, even to the extent that she would dismount outside the house and pretend to find a stone in Poppy's hoof. If Larry was in the garden, he was bound to have heard the hooves clapping along the road.

Poppy took the saddle and bridle easily, standing quietly as Susan mounted and adjusted her stirrups and girth. Then, squeezing her legs gently, the well-trained Poppy moved into a forward walk. They were hardly out of the farm entrance when the first flakes of snow began to fall.

"Just my luck!" muttered Susan but instantly decided that there was too much involved to abandon the ride. Poppy surely has often experienced snow, even on a polo field. The thought of Poppy not having experienced snow on a road, however, did pass through her mind but immediately discarded the thought as silly; of course, a horse of that age must have walked on many a slippery road.

Having walked a few hundred yards Susan broke Poppy into a trot, thinking that if she was going to do the round trip she had planned she had better get a move on before the snow made things difficult. The Manor house was in a dip in the middle of the village and normally Susan would not trot a horse downhill, but time was now a factor. She considered that Larry was unlikely to be in the garden as it was now snowing but she would keep to her plan. As she came up to the manor gates her easing back on the reins coincided with a delivery lorry passing that also must have been short on time to complete deliveries. While braking when he saw the horse, the lorry skidded and knocked into the horse sending both Susan and the horse sliding through the snow. The lorry managed to stop, and the anxious driver jumped out to help Susan up; fortunately, the snow had prevented any skin grazing. Both Susan and the driver ran over to the horse that was struggling on the road, its hooves sending flurries of snow as it writhed on its side.

Hearing the commotion, Larry appeared through the manor house gate asking what had happened, even though the scene was obvious.

"Are you OK, Sue?" asked Larry putting an arm on her shoulder.

"Yes, I'm OK, Larry but I'm not sure about Poppy. You wanted to see Poppy when she arrived, but I never thought it would be like this." Susan finished the sentence with tears in her eyes.

The lorry driver pocketed his mobile, saying, "I've contacted the police and ambulance and they're on their way."

"I'm OK, so I don't need an ambulance but it's a vet that the horse needs" as Susan took out her own mobile, adding to the lorry driver, "Can you cancel the ambulance?" Whereupon the driver dug out his phone again.

The police arrived about the same time as the vet that Susan always used. He immediately went to Poppy who was less frantic now and more resigned to laying quietly in the snow. The vet injected a sedative saying that it might help her to feel ready to stand up again.

"Can we try and sweep some of this snow away from the horse so it can get a better grip on the road."

Larry rushed back to the manor to get a broom while the two police officers started clearing the snow from around the horse with their feet.

"Come on, Poppy, get up!" shouted Susan while prodding the horse on the rump; "Get up, get up!"

Just as Larry appeared with the broom, Poppy did manage to make a powerful struggle and got up albeit with one of its forelegs caught in the reins. As Susan moved forward to lift the leg out of the reins the vet said, "hold on, there's something not right here." Standing next to Poppy's flank he moved his hand down the pony's hind leg at which Poppy then gave a big flinch that made the vet jump back. "I think we may have a serious injury here; could be a strain, a ligament or even a break. We'll have to have her back at the surgery for an x-ray." Adding, "Can you go back and get your trailer and bring Poppy to the surgery now?"

Larry quickly added, "It's OK, Sue; I'll hold on to Poppy while you get the trailer."

One of the police officers had been interviewing the lorry driver but the other one chipped in, "I tell you what, as this is urgent for the animal I'll run you back to get the trailer as it's going to take a few minutes for my mate to write everything down.

Susan returned with the trailer and very slowly Poppy was persuaded to limp in, almost on three legs; the other seemed to be raised painfully.

The x-ray at the surgery confirmed the vet's worst fears that Poppy had indeed a small break in her hind leg where the lorry had hit her.

Holding up the x-ray to the light to show Susan, the vet removed his glasses and said, "You basically have two choices, Sue. As it's a small break the bone may eventually heal, but the horse is over twenty and the healing will be slower with no certainty that she will ever be sound again. Obviously, I can give her something to relieve the pain. Alternatively, considering the pain that Poppy may be in and the fact that she is over twenty, it may be sensible to put her down."

Susan looked deep into the vet's eyes wondering if he may come up with a third option. She had insured Poppy when she picked her up from Jill for both treatment or death. There was a lingering silence as Susan realised that it wasn't an easy decision to make.

A Fair Day's Run

I like it in the morning when the sun streaks through the crack
and my stable door swings open wide to blaze the gloom
with light.
My sugar beat's been mixed with oats and carrots from the sack;
a super pony breakfast that has perked me up just right.

So now it's time to wonder what my owner has in store.
Will it be a woodland ride or splashing through the sea,
or sometimes trudging through the bog or canter round the moor,
or boxing up to ride the Downs and gallop feeling free?

It's not the box; we're riding out, not even to the coast.
That means it's just a mile or two to reach the village pub.
"Sunday lunch," my owner says; she likes her Sunday roast,
but mostly what she swallows down are pints of ale, not grub!

A couple hours of boredom and she staggers having drank.
Forgets to lose the hitching rope but mounts up; yes, you guessed.
She doesn't give me any choice as hard she spurs my flank
and off comes the hitching rail full spread across my chest.

I seize my chance to have some fun, my rider now quite drunk.
I grasp the bit and have my head and gallop to the fete.
The village fair is in full swing with stalls and tents and junk.

Like Boadicea, I run amok with bunting in full spate.
Crash go the tables with some squealings from the mix.
Hamburgers flying and candyfloss flipped.
Prize-winning marrow gets a knocking for a six
as the cake stall goes mushy while the stilt-walker's tripped.

Guy-ropes on tents make a tuning out of twang,
marquees, gazebos deflating to the ground.
That Rolls in its class has taken quite a prang
and the brass band makes quite a different sort of sound.

My puff has made me tired, but I've had my run of fame.
Surrounded by the chaos, as the fists are flaying air,
I munch the tasty doughnut that got caught up in my mane.
What a memory I will cherish of the day I ran the fair.

A Sign of the Times

As the shaft of morning light streaks through the stable gloom
I hear the clink of bucket, the swish of stable broom.
    The morning chorus mingles with the neighs of waiting steeds,
    waiting for our breakfast, waiting for our feeds.

Bang goes the bolt as the top door opens wide.
Clang goes the kick-bolt as the groom appears inside
    with a bucket of sugar beet, carrots, oats and hay;
    a manger full of sheer delights to start this sunny day.

With breakfast now inside me my groom is working hard.
Then a halter to my collar and I'm led into the yard.
    Frantic with the dandy brush, curry comb and sponge
    and leading to the riding school and ready for my lunge.

Round and around in circles, a walk, a trot and halt
then perfectly the other way without a slip or fault.
    On with the saddle and tighten up the girth;
    I'm so excited that I can't contain my mirth.

Up jumps my rider filling stirrups full of boot.
Off up the driveway and through the gate we shoot.
    Trotting up the roadway where the traffic makes a threat
    Can't wait to reach the bridleway and the gallop I will get.

There be our bridleway a yard or two ahead
but no, my rider stops us by that sign that's painted red.
The way is barred, the sign is bold and none of words say,
"please",
just, "KEEP OFF, KEEP OUT, Five Thousand Pounds;
Foot and Mouth Disease".

Celebration

Martina tied up the bulging hay net over Sofia's stable door and turned to Georgio with a heavy sigh, "Well darling, that's probably the last hay net that She's gonna have before she foals down."

"Well," retorted Georgio, "The vet did say she wasn't certain and that it could be any day now. Anyway, I'll relieve you at three in the morning as you're keeping an eye on her 'till then."

"Yup, I'll just pop in and brew a coffee flask before my watch and you'd better get some sleep now." Martina dragged herself to the villa kitchen followed by Georgio who immediately bid her goodnight, bounding the stairs two at a time.

The couple had bought the Tuscan villa, near Treppio, four years before and had spent most of their savings building stables and a small barn. They had been surprised at how expensive the fencing materials had been to secure the five small paddocks amounting to 22 acres, or 10 hectares as the agent had described them. Martina's mother was Italian and lived nearby in Florence and it was on the many holidays to Tuscany spent with her English father that she met up with Georgio, the son of a Tuscan farmer.

Martina made a flask of coffee realising that she would probably need the input of caffeine if she was to stay awake till the early hours. Returning to the stable she settled down on a hay bale in the stable corner and poured a cup of her piping hot drink. Looking at Sofia, Martina reflected that surely Sofia couldn't get much larger with the foal inside; it must arrive today or tomorrow at the latest. It was a warm evening and Martina felt a cool feeling run down her back and shoulders as she leaned back against the cold stone blocks of the stable wall. She had watched Sofia eating her hay over many years and this night was no different to the extent that Martina's eyes closed, and she went into a satisfying, well-needed snooze after her exhausting day.

With her mind just beginning to enjoy a dream she was suddenly awakened by Sofia going down onto the straw bed. Martina quickly became alert, thinking this could be it. Sofia did a few rolls on the straw and then stood up giving a severe shake to get the odd bits of tickling straw off her back. Then after a minute Sofia started to shake; this was a shaking that Martina had never seen before and sweat started to appear all over her flank.

"This is not right," Martina muttered to herself and with no hesitation pulled out her mobile from her pocket and phoned the vet. She knew there was always a vet on 24 hours' notice. Aurora, the vet on duty, answered immediately and, after hearing Martina's description of Sofia's shaking, said that she would come out instantly and see the horse.

As Martina put the phone back in her pocket, Sofia, still shaking and now quite violently, went down onto the straw and started thrashing around. I need Georgio here, she thought to herself and ran back to the villa, shouting, "Georgio, Georgio, help! Come quickly!" as she entered.

Georgio was already jumping down the stairs, still in his jeans and they both ran out to the stable. As they opened the stable door, they found Sofia still thrashing about and shaking violently, lying down. Then, quite suddenly, she stopped, the shaking stopped, her head laid back on the straw and her eyes glazed over in that recognisable state of death.

"Oh, hell, Georgio, she's gone!"

"Yes," replied Georgio. "looks like it. That's really sad as she seemed in the best of health just a few hours ago."

As they stared at Sofia's body and tried to take in the catastrophic happening, they heard Aurora's car pull up by the stable. They both turned to Aurora as she speedily got out of the car and told her that she was too late, and that Sofia had died.

"When did she die?" asked Aurora.

"Oh, just a couple of minutes ago," replied Georgio as Martina held her head in her hands, tears rolling down her cheeks.

Aurora, pushed past Georgio into the stable and, opening her bag up, checked there was no pulse, pulled out a scalpel and proceeded to slice a deep cut up Sofia's abdomen. Fluid poured out from the wound and amidst the fluid, some blood and a placenta. The foal became clear within the gaping slice of the uterus and she extracted the body, head and dangling legs from within. Martina stopped crying as she realised what the vet was doing.

With a few sharp slaps and some CPR on the foal's chest the foal started to move, cough out some fluid and then breathe. As the vet started to monitor the foal's heartbeat with her stethoscope, delving into her bag for an antibiotic injection she said to Martina, "Run quickly to the villa and bring a clean bowl, please."

The foal was now trying to stand up and as Martina rushed back with the bowl, Aurora said, "Yes, that's ideal, now milk the mare into the bowl."

"But," replied Martina, "the mare is dead."

"Yes," answered Aurora, "but that special milk, we call colostrum, is still there and the foal needs it. Go ahead, you'll see the milk will still flow when you milk her."

And to Martina's surprise, the milk did flow and was given to the leggy filly foal.

A few days later Georgio asked Martina what they should name their miracle filly foal.

Martina paused in thought for a moment, then said, "I think we should call her, 'Chelly' because the Italian for celebration is celebrazione and Italians pronounce the 'C' as a 'Ch'."

Spring Cheer

Such a bouncing in my striding as I trot around the field;
    There's a feeling of elation as the sun shines brighter still
and the bursting buds of Springtime splash a colour round
the Weald,
    while the other ponies frolic feeling frisky for a thrill.

Break into a canter, do a jump or two and rear.
    Sniff the air expectantly as herbs in pastures bloom.
Munch that lush-green grassy swathe that decks the dawn of year.
    Get behind me winter; be gone you demon gloom.

But now the ground is harder as the mud will hibernate
    and that farmer with a roller has erased the cloddy mire.
The daylight starts so Early and the sunset lingers late.
    There's a passion in my living with a 'lust-for-life' desire.

My term of months are over when my foal will bring delight
    but those humans make me nervous like the last horse here
        on Earth.
They come out in the dead of dark, their torches gouge the night,
    hoping that my time has come when I will give them birth.

"Nothing doing, owner dear; you'll have to wait and see.
Don't you know us pregnant mares are shy and shun a show?"
I'll wait until they've gone back in and mind and womb agree,
when Spring will nourish one more foal whose birth is
mine to know.

The moment of my fortune passes silently and sure
as the leggy, lanky lassie lies there steaming dressed in silk.
The miracle of standing; first a stagger then some more
while she celebrates the moment with a tot of creamy milk.

February's Pony

February's Pony is often rather impish
    nosing into feed bins when he didn't really ought;
chewing at the tails of the pony friends when peckish,
    keeping just a wisp away when it's time to be caught.

Naughty little pony that is searching round the fences,
    trotting up and down the line to seek a tiny gap.
Busting through the barbed wire, hedges even densest;
    that agile, escapologist your energy he will sap.

Down the road he's trotting in the middle of the dark night,
    grazing on the verges with excitement in his veins.
Fortunately, a motorist reveals him in the headlight,
    shoos him to a garden, shuts the gate and ties with chains.

Frantic garden owner wakes to find him in the morning
    lying on the roses with hoof marks in the lawn.
Dressing gown and shoes on, the owner tries some calling
    but all this sleepy pony does is give a noisy yawn.

Phone call to the local yard reveals the pony's missing
    Trailer comes and picks him up returning to his home.
"You naughty little pony; no, you don't deserve my kissing!"
    He bucks and rears and gallops off never more to roam…
    pigs might fly!

Now he's rolling on his back feet kicking in the air.
Trouble is he's on a rock and rips his rug to shreds.
Up he gets and gives a shake yet doesn't seem to care;
just more money from my purse for needle and
some threads.

Now it's started snowing and he trots to frozen lake,
skids along, exciting this and slides along to stop.
The ice gives way so down he goes but clambers out to shake;
lucky to be only cold but least he's out on top.

He loves his weekly wash and groom with coat all clean
and bright,
then turn him out, he rolls in mud; why did I waste
my time?
The long dark nights are fading fast as spring brings in more light.
He frolics even more so now; his life's a pantomime!

The Carrot

There's a snowman in the garden and it's looking straight at me
with an elongated carrot such as forms his orange nose.
I've been chewing up some hay and been munching at my tea
and the ground is all so frosted, and my water trough just froze.

That carrot looks so pretty and so enticingly at me
so, try some levitation but it doesn't move an inch.
I strain my neck across the hedge to try if I can be
just a little closer to that root; that nose I'd like to pinch!

Every moment as I watch, it beckons me to bite.
More orangey and fatter, bigger; crammed with fuller taste.
Luminescent orange life raft in an Artic full of white…
I long to be the rescue plane to snap it up in haste.

Walking 'long the paddock edge to find the garden gate
but the rusty, little sliding bolt has frozen in its cot.
Breathing deeply, huffing, puffing as I blow the breath of fate;
low behold, the ice has gone. It slides the slimy slot!

No one in the house I see; my owner's gone away.
    Hoofprints make impressions that will tell a tale of me.
A beeline for that carrot; will it be all that I pray?
    Canter, frolic, kick and buck and headlong full of glee.

Arriving at the snowman with a skid and full of mirth,
    his eyes screwed up, his carrot twitched, he sneezed for what
    it's worth.
"Aaaahhhhhh tishew!" went the snowman as the snow flowed
all around…
    I never found my carrot as it flipped into the ground.

Flies

Those pesky little creatures are the bane of my life,
    frequently flitting furtively from dunghill to food.
I've even seen my owner wield a fly-swat in strife
    but they're just too quick for her; she must be shrewd.
A godsend that I'm blessed with such a hairy tail.
    I don't even think about swishing them away.
Whenever there's a tickle, my reflex is to flail
    and any little varmint is lucky to end the day.
There are house flies, bot flies, horse flies and more;
    butterflies and dragonflies don't bother me much.
It's those blood-sucking, egg-laying culprits galore
    that upset my summertime, sunny days, as such.
Another reflex action when my wither makes a twitch.
    Don't even have to think of it while munching at the grass.
They drink the fluid from my eyes which then start to itch.
    All day long until the dark and then the pain will pass.
Oil of citronella my owner often tries
    to find a way to rid me of these brats.
A fly-fringe was used to cover my eyes
    but useless at night when invaded by gnats.
A fly-mask was always better than most
    allowed me to see and stopped the sun's glare.
But one night in darkness I walked into a post
    and the vet bill was more than my owner could bear.
The Aussies are clever, they put corks on their hats
    and seldom a fly will venture through those.

But here in the summer we give them a splat
    and long for the winter when flies can get froze!
So, the solution to that buzzing, annoying sound
    is an eight-legged creature that devours them a lot.
Breed lots of hungry spiders so their sticky webs abound
    so many flies will disappear; we'll never need to swat!

The Prisoner of Gender

Filthy, dirty hovel that has never seen a muck fork;
corrugated rust sheets letting in the rain;
        muscles shaking coldly,
        vermin creeping boldly,
the law that lets this happen cannot visualise my pain.

Pennies are the money that keep me in limbo;
keep me in a dungeon, dingy and dark.
        There's muck on show
        where my hooves sink low
and I dream of the freedom caressed by the lark.

With head bent low and ears on the rafters,
feeling very lonely in this dank, black hole;
        shaking to the horror
        that I'll be here tomorro'
and praying that this human god will take my soul.

Very little water and feeling oh so thirsty
my life is full of sadness for these human faults.
        Urine making puddles,
        never any cuddles,
so, pity all the yearlings who were born as simple colts.

Batty, biddy owner as a frugal keeper,
making sure his money doesn't give me any scope.
    Longing for some leather tack;
    trot out on a bridle track;
all my aspirations fondly cultivate my hope.

The Commons and the bureaucrats couldn't give a damn,
full of dull endeavour and a lack of thrust and clout.
    The law is oh so feeble
    'cause currently it's legal
to leave me in a prison, in the dark and not let out.

My Love for Him

Well-groomed Joe has the strength of a Titan;
a battery of muscles ripple furrows 'long his side.
Eyes ever glisten,
ears always listen,
head held high and stature full of pride.

Full of masculinity, his breeding from the best,
his hair so groomed that my fingers like caress.
He slurps when he drinks
but emotion binds our links
and my absolute devotion for him seals my love no less.

Then that sunny morning when we're strolling down
the road,
he espies another female lying, lounging in a field.
"Joe, you behave,
for I know what you crave."
But his beeline for that damsel was a strength I had to yield.

Up jumps the lady as his pounding feet approached,
wide-eyed and staring as she stands there in the nude
"Joe, you naughty boy!"
As the female seems all coy.
She turns and runs much faster as she must have thought
him rude.

Returning to our amble down the lane and to the pub,
I swallowed back my anger as I love my Joe, of course.
It was with my greatest pleasure
that I tied him up with leather,
as my randy Joe's a stallion, yes, my loving Joe's a horse.

A Flipping Good Job Too!

That pony they call 'Trojan' keeps on kicking out at me.
If I find a patch of lush green grass he always comes to see.
Just like a big spoilt baby he will push me out the way
and grabs the best of grazing and the sweetest pick of hay.

It doesn't matter how spaced out the piles of hay are spread
that Trojan brute will chase us round so none of us get fed.
And when the owners come with food and buckets
all prepared
that Trojan beast will bite and kick and make us all so scared.

One evening as we gathered in a copse down near the stream,
while Trojan stood and dosed way off, we conjured up
our scheme.
Ash Wednesday and Shrove Tuesday brings the pancake
race again
but this village has a special race on horseback down the lane.

All is set, the vicar's here, reporters from the press;
the Mums and Dads all bring their kids, most in their fancy dress.
There's frying pans and lots of dough all flattened
and pre-cooked
and some prizes for the winners and a list of entries booked.

First the little children flick their pancakes in the air
followed by the Mums and Dads who cheat as they do dare.
    Now it's time that special race where saddles not allowed.
    Our riders jump on top of us with frying pans all proud.

Off go the riders flipping freely as they race,
pancakes flying everywhere; one even hits a face!
    But we have plans for Trojan as we gallop past the pond,
    we push him off the roadway, so he tosses in beyond.

So that selfish, bully gelding got the damper he deserves.
He's gone quite meek and gentle-like, not getting on our nerves.
    And so, the morale's obvious; from the horse's mouth we get
    Don't push and grab or bully or you'll end up very wet!

Your Horse May Be Listening

"Hey, Dobbin, that was blooming painful when that vet shoved the needle in."

"Yeah, Queenie, and I wasn't too impressed with the farrier when one of the nails went into the sensitive part of my hoof."

"Did the vet apologize when I jumped? 'Course he didn't. They never do. What about the farrier, did he say he was sorry?"

"Did he hell! No, all they ever do is curse. But I tell you what. I heard them talking about some animal they call 'Turkey'."

"Turkey, Dobbin, what were they saying then?"

"Well, Queenie, it was most strange. It seems this creature hasn't got fur like us but has a transparent skin like plastic. One of them was saying she was going to 'defrost' it."

"What does 'defrost' mean, Dobbin?"

"Well, Queenie, I'm not sure, but they talked about letting it stand for 24 hours."

"Oh, Dobbin, that's so cruel. Even I can't stand for 24 hours."

"Of course, it's cruel Queenie, but I tell you, worse was to come. A few days later I heard her asking, who wanted the 'drumsticks'."

"Drumsticks, Dobbin? What do you mean?"

"Queenie, these humans have extraordinary powers. It seems they can make this turkey produce any implement they want."

"Oh, you mean like the goose that laid the golden egg?"

"Exactly, Queenie. This is when they must be short of sticks to play their drums. Next it will be that they're short of saddles or lunging reins. Where will it all end?"

"Dobbin, you're frightening me."

"Yeah, but hold on Queenie, there's more. Apparently, they're able to get hold of a parson's nose."

"You mean they actually cut off the nose of a parson?"

"Queenie, I have to be honest with you. That's the only way they're going to get such a nose, and, yes, I agree with you. These humans have a very low regard for their fellow human beings. Of course, the noseless parson probably survives the amputation but obviously he won't smell anymore!"

"I've never smelt a parson."

"Queenie, get with it; there's more intrigue to this."

"What do you mean Dobbin?"

"Oh, Queenie, it's obvious. They're cloning the nose to produce loads of parsons."

"Why do they want lots of parsons, Dobbin?"

"Well, it seems, Queenie, that Parsons are the 'do-gooders' of human society; they're able to call on magic to make everything right!"

"Wow, Dobbin! If only we had some parsons working magic to make everything right for us here in this field."

"Queenie, you and I are the last things in the minds of these humans at this time of year. Humans give presents to each other. We're not even in the running! The most we can expect is a few extra carrots for supper."

"Dobbin you're so defeatist! I'm sure there are hundreds of horse lovers out there that would give food and presents to us. What would you like for a present, Queenie?"

"Well, sometimes I see my rider all dressed up when she's not riding and she wears high heeled shoes and looks very pretty, so I would like the farrier to put high-heeled shoes on me next time. What about you, Dobbin, what would you like for a present?"

"Well, when my rider comes back from a ride she always sits down. I am fed up with standing up or lying down; I would like a chair so I can sit down like her!"

1st

Summer Ponytimes

All terms at an end, the holidays brim
so brushed and so washed and ponywise trim.
    My rider so loves me, hugs me and she
    does cherish the summer two thousand and three.

Gymkhana the show when everyone clapped
after the fence I only just tapped.
    Head over heels, my rider flew free;
    that summer of August two thousand and three.

That Pony Club camp when a bee stung my thigh,
campfire sausages flying on high,
    wash lines and guy-ropes as tents bow to me;
    such havoc in heaven the summer '03.

That hack to remember, when given my head,
I galloped in front and never got lead.
    Wind hissing my ears, heart pounding in glee;
    that summer of August two thousand and three.

The fancy-dress class she draped me in white,
put wings on my thighs; a Pegasus knight!
        The rosette was red, three judges agree;
        my happiest summer two thousand and three.

The obstacle race was fun to the core,
battens, balloons, relays and more.
        My owner fell flat with the sack round her knee
        crawling in last, that summer '03.

Chase-me-Charlie was never a test,
my first round was noisy; I gave it my best.
        Domino fences destroyed in my spree;
        I relish the summer two thousand and three.

What memories lurk in my rider's bright brain?
Perhaps she will think that, in me, they wane.
No telly, no books, my mind is set free;
my souvenir summer two thousand and three.

A Hoof Problem – a children's story

Brandy, the poodle, was on her way home from school when she came across her friend Pompy the pony. Pompy was lying down under a tree with big tears rolling down his cheeks.

"Oh, Pompy," exclaimed Brandy. "Why are you crying?" But Pompy didn't answer.

"Pompy," she asked again, "What has happened? Didn't you go to school today?"

Pompy sniffed and then gave a deep sigh. "Oh, yes," Pompy sniffed, "I went to school but today we had to do writing and I couldn't hold the pen in my hoof. I'll never be able to write if I can't hold a pen." Pompy again burst out in tears.

"Oh Pompy," said Brandy pulling out a large tissue from under her woolly coat, "Here, take this and dry your eyes. There must be something we can do to help you write. Come on, let's walk home together." Pompy rose to his feet and walked slowly back across the fields with his head hanging low and the occasional tear dropping onto the grass.

As they walked through one of the farm gates Brandy suddenly stopped and said, "I know what we'll do. We'll go and see my uncle Lambi. He's a professor at the university and usually knows the answers to everything."

"I don't see how he can change my hoof so it can hold a pen," said Pompy with a dejected look.

"Oh, come on," shouted Brandy. He only lives at the bottom of the village and he'll be there now."

"I suppose I've got nothing else to do. OK then." Off they set to the end of the village.

Professor Lambi was quite grey round his whiskers but was the only Labrador dog to have lived in the village for so long. He lived in the big manor house and everyone turned to him when they had a problem. Brandy opened the latch on the heavy iron gate which squeaked noisily as it opened. The pair went in with their eyes open wide in wonder at the grand entrance. Brandy made sure to shut the gate behind them and then tugged hard on the big iron rod that hung down the side of the heavy front door.

"Hello!" came a call from behind them and Brandy and Pompy jumped with fright while the bell sounded from deep within the house. Turning around they were confronted with Professor Lambi strolling round from the side of the house with a spade.

"Just been doing a bit of digging," puffed the Professor. "I'm always pleased to have an excuse to have a rest from digging."

"Hello Uncle," said Brandy, and Pompy rather nervously stammered a hello sir.

"And what can I do for you?" asked the Professor.

"Well, er, um." Brandy was a bit nervous now she was confronted with her uncle, face to face. "Well, Uncle, it's like this. Pompy here has been crying and is very sad because he wants to write but he can't hold a pen in his hoof."

Professor Lambi looked hard at Pompy and then down to his hooves and back up to his face where another big tear was beginning to run down from each eye.

"Yes, I see the problem," he said. "This is not going to be easy."

There were a few moments of complete silence as they could see Professor Lambi thinking hard as to how he could solve the problem. After a minute or two he broke the silence saying, "Of course you know that all problems can be solved. I have an idea for this one. Go home and come back and see me tomorrow. I'll see what I can do."

"Oh, thank you, thank you uncle," said Brandy with an excited smile on her face and even Pompy cheered up a little, pricking up his ears. The pair returned through the iron gate, waving goodbye to the professor as he turned and seemed to go back to his gardening.

Professor Lambi went back to his garden, stuck the spade hard in the ground and left it there as he wandered into his large, wooden garden shed. For several hours and deep into the night, passers-by could hear loud banging and other noises coming from the shed and very late at night the professor went back to his house to bed.

The next morning after breakfast the professor carried two large, heavy cardboard boxes out to the shed and then, an hour later, sighed to himself, "There, all finished at last."

"Knock, knock," Brandy rapped on Pompy's door and shouted, "Pompy, are you there?"

Pompy came immediately and the two set off for the end of the village. Entering through the heavy iron gates, the squeak of the gate again alerted the professor who came around the corner from the garden.

"This way," he said excitedly, with a big smile on his face, and led the two around to the shed. The shed door creaked as the three went into the gloomy inside. As the professor switched on the light the pair gazed in wonder.

"What is it?" asked Brandy.

"It's so big" said Pompy. "I thought you were making a special pen for me to write with. This doesn't look like a pen."

In front of them was what appeared to be a few steps of a small staircase but each step had been sawn up into lots of little bits. Each bit of step had a letter or number on it.

"It's a pony-size keyboard," said the Professor. "You will have the best writing in the school because as you type with your hooves it goes onto the computer screen and you can print out everything you write. The computer even corrects your mistakes and spelling. The computer and printer were old ones that I don't need any more; the only thing I had to make was the keyboard."

On Monday, with a big smile on his face, Pompy pulled the writing machine to school in a cart and everyone was so amazed at how well it worked that Professor Lambi was asked to make more for all the other ponies in the class.

Books for Loan
MARKET NEWS
UNITED STATES NOW AT WAR WITH GERMANY

Bank on Taking the Right Decision

Hitler's rise to power hadn't gone unnoticed even in our little market town but life was good; plenty of food, and my family even had an allotment so fresh vegetables were a bonus. Indeed, Dad often gave some of the produce to the James's, our next-door neighbours. They would often respond by taking us somewhere in their Ford car that Mr James had bought second hand for £85. I remember him walking excitedly to the bank and drawing out 17 large, white five-pound notes which he proudly showed me before buying the car. I'd never seen these notes before.

Ronald, our milkman, always fascinated me, well, not exactly him, but 'Flicker', his horse. How on earth did Flicker know when to stop and when to move on with the milk cart? Several times I tried to work out whether Flicker was using his ears to the clink of the bottles or whether he was able to see Ron's walking back and forth. I had to rule out the latter as Flicker wore blinkers so couldn't see sideways and, anyway, he never moved his head. Eventually I concluded that Flicker was able to hear the difference between empty and full milk bottles and a rare "Woa" or "Wok-on" from Ron's puffing breath.

So, it was a sad day when I answered the door to Ron's expected knock on a Friday to pay his milk bill and he said that this was his last day as he was retiring. As I handed over the five and sixpence he said, "Don't worry about your milk for next week as there's another chap going to do the rounds only he's going to have one of these new fandangled electric vans."

"But Ron," I said, "it won't be the same, and anyway, I will miss seeing Flicker."

"Oh" replied Ron, "Flicker's retiring as well though I'm not sure where he's going yet."

Ron could see I was getting a bit agitated when I asked, "Ron, you won't have him put down, will you?"

"No, never." he replied. "He's been a faithful buddy for over fifteen years; he has earned, and deserves, a peaceful and happy retirement as well. He's eighteen now, yu know."

I hesitated for a moment in thought as he handed me the receipt. "Ron, if you can't find anywhere for Flicker to go, can I have him? There's a large shed on Dad's allotment and plenty of greenery he can be spoilt with and I can also get him hay from farmer Jones down Flitterbrook Lane."

"Well, now Miss Roberts, that's a very kind offer and, yes, that will certainly solve my retirement worries. We don't need to have any paperwork as I know you well and could even pop by and see Flicker at your allotment occasionally. I'll bring him around tomorrow afternoon if that's OK?"

"Yes, fantastic!" I could hardly control my enthusiasm.

At four o'clock on Saturday afternoon, Ron duly appeared leading Flicker, now without blinkers or any harness. After a little chat and useful advice by Ron he shook my hand and I noticed tears in his eyes as he turned away, walking slowly back down the road.

From day one Flicker settled into his new routine and I managed to get onto a half day shift working at the library, which gave me more time to spend with my new friend. A week later I was able to buy a second-hand saddle and bridle. Flicker didn't blink an eyelid as I placed them on him. He was so used to having harness put on him every day that he never flinched at all. Ron never mentioned if Flicker had ever been ridden but he just stood quite still as I got on his back. Oh, yes, he would walk ahead but only if I said "Wok-on," as Ron used to say it. It took several weeks before Flicker learned to associate my heels nudging his flank with "Wok-on" and after a couple of months I could dispense with the verbal command and he would move forward, responding to my heel nudge alone.

The bank was next to our library with an alleyway between, having been converted from an old stable yard the bank still had a large grassy yard area behind on which bank staff sometimes parked a car. The bank manager, Mr MacDonald, was a bit hesitant when I first asked him, but eventually agreed that I could occasionally leave Flicker in the yard providing I made the back entrance secure so he couldn't get out. This allowed me to ride to work for my shift and ride home afterwards.

It was on one such occasion that I rode up to the library noticing a car outside with its engine running and a man at the wheel reading a paper. I dismounted, led Flicker up the alleyway and into the yard. My shift was only going to be three hours, but I still put the padlock on the heavy iron gates and, as usual, went in via the library back entrance.

I had hardly stepped into the library when the other librarian, Julia, was exclaiming that something was happening out at the front. I rushed over to hear the bells of a police car that swerved in front of the parked car that I had previously noticed. Four policemen jumped out of the car; one confronted the driver in the parked car while the other three rushed into the bank.

"Wow!" I exclaimed to Julia, "there must have been a robbery going on at the bank."

"Yes," replied Julia, "That car outside seems to have been something to do with it; a get-away car perhaps?"

"Well," I surmised, "They obviously didn't get away as that bobby has got that driver out of the car and is frisking him. And look, those other three policemen are coming out of the bank with those two chaps in handcuffs."

A second police car had turned up by now and all were bundled into the two cars and obviously on their way to the police station.

It was a couple of hours later when Mr MacDonald and another man in a suit came to my desk. "Hello, Miss Roberts, this is inspector Dodge from the local police station." I shook his extended hand as he smiled and nodded. Mr MacDonald then passed me a big bunch of flowers from behind his back, saying, "If it hadn't been for your horse in the back yard, we wouldn't have caught the robbers."

"How was that, then?" I asked.

"Well," replied Inspector Dodge, "Seems that Mr MacDonald, here, normally leaves the back gates open but you padlocked them. When we arrived at the front entrance the only way they could escape was through the back entrance and you had made that impossible. Those two blighters couldn't escape anywhere; they had to come quietly."

At the weekend the local paper had a front-page writeup about the robbery with a photo. The paper's photographer had taken a photo of Flicker and I standing proudly at the iron gates.

From a Winter's Field

I startle at the rattle of the gate into my patch
as a stranger with a pony lets it go and what a match!
  It's a lovely skewbald filly
  with a name that sounds like Tilly,
so, we sniff and snort and rub our necks; at last a mutual scratch!

For Christmas Eve, I can't deceive; this is my greatest joy,
for I'm a piebald gelding, yes, a lonely pony boy.
  Many humans never realise
  that companions we idealize
and my best of Christmas presents is a pony not a toy.

Now Christmas's gone and winter's here, the chill can give me pain
My owner's put a rug on me, and Tilly has the same.
  They keep us warm
  and oft get torn;
that barbed wire fence, a bad idea, to fence me from the lane.

My water trough has crust of ice; so, I cannot drink.
And then my owner breaks a hole to make a water chink.
  Winter feed and scented hay
  delivered to me every day,
but all too oft is put on the ground and blown away, I think.

My field a swathe of whiteness as the snow lays all around,
a pretty sight to wonder as the snow-froth deadens sound.
  Then Spring arrives,
  the sun connives
to melt, warm up and grow again the grass from in the ground.

An Equine Affaire!

Coloured pony, 'Bank's Celest'
felt quite hard done by, he'd been messed.
"An upstart colt," the breeder, said
"Keep him stabled, under fed."

As time passed by, and oft sold on,
Celest became a stallion;
but all the mares on every farm
were kept away well out of harm.

For several months Celest had seen
an attractive mare with coat so sheen.
She also noticed him o'er the fence
with snort and winks and love so tense.

Celest kept himself aware,
the farmer regularly lacked in care.
Sometimes failing to close field gates
or forgetting the farmers' market dates.

At last one day there came the fault
when the farmer forgot to close the bolt.
Celest seized the chance and galloped through
with bucks and snorts and a hullabaloo.

Over the field and, finding the mare,
Celest rubbed his nose on her flank with care.
Several months later the mare gave birth,
a filly foal, salt of the Earth!

Following the 9/11 terrorist plane attacks on the USA in 2001 the USA responded by attacking Afghanistan in order to dismantle Al-Qaeda and remove the Taliban from power. Later, yellow food parcels were dropped by parachute.

I'm Also an Afghan

You can look and you can see me
In the papers, on the TV,
Walking 'cross your screen in London town
with a burden of a bundle
and some chattels very humble
and you wonder why my load won't bring me down.

Just a donkey you may say,
And you recognise my neigh,
but do you ever sense my sorry plight?
Explosions draw my tears,
as they're louder with my ears,
and the smell of semtex, TNT and foul cordite.

From Kabul to Kandahar,
as the missiles come from far,
and my master takes to mountains to conceal.
Trekking over ridge, through pass,
quite bereft of any grass,
and the straps cut deep to bleed and never heal.

From Herat to Khaybar Pass
lay six hundred miles so sparse,
where weeps the yellow packs of food for man.
Is there someone hears my plea
for some hay and food for me,
a simple donkey beast, a true Afghan?

Horse Arrest

My grazing's getting short and sparse
with poison plants entwined.
Why don't my owners sow more grass
for horse, like me; be kind?

Now I see a chink in hedge
delicious roadside verge.
I squeeze myself into a wedge
to leave this pasture dirge.

Freedom, freedom, free at last,
the air alive with hooves.
loads of grass, this verge is vast,
a gallop, trot and moves.

Having munched, I've had enough;
I've yearned for many a year.
So out of form I'm losing my puff,
escaped, and my owners, I fear.

But here by the road is a cottage so quaint;
wisteria abounds round the porch.
The windows are leaded with outline in paint;
inside they are flashing a torch.

A burglar, perhaps? I trot through the door
suspect he is committing a crime.
Surprise on his face as he's rifling the store;
he turns to the kitchen in time.

Hooves slide along to a halt on the floor,
a slippery change to pastures I know.
Rushing in, he slams the oak door
but my bodyweight gives it a blow.

Splinters, pots and pans abound,
catastrophe of kitchen ware.
Dodging to a doorway he stumbles to ground.
Then, on his feet and climbing the stair.

Challenge me not, as jumping I've done,
so up I leap with five at a stride.
The landing carpet feeds me some fun,
and under the bed he's trying to hide.

With hooves on the floor, front on the bed,
I pound hard down to shake from his nest.
Out he crawls, intentions all shed,
and Police arrive with warrant arrest.

So, if you own a cottage with aged beams involved,
consider this story and all that has passed.
All cottages inherit a crime to be solved;
just call in a horse as horse sense is vast.

Rustle to Freedom

OK, I'm just an ordinary pony you may say, born on Dartmoor, bought at the auctions for a knock down price and then carted off in a horsebox to that green and pleasant land they call Sussex. Well, my days as a foal were quite enjoyable as I must admit that my owners were apparently, quite rich, at least that is what I heard folk say when they were walking around the stables. Yes, you might say I was pampered but I learnt to follow their rules and not take advantage of situations, like being given titbits when out in the field. Some of the other horses would get quite aggressive and push each other to get the hand-outs but I found, if I held back, the owners would notice and give me a few extras.

This happy life went on for about three years. I'm not sure what a year is but for the last few months I've been hearing them outside my stable saying things like "break-in", "saddle" and "lunging". I didn't know what these words meant but it wasn't long before I found out, as one day, they took me out in my head collar and started putting bags of straw on my back. Well, of course I didn't much care for that but when they kept popping a few pony cubes into my mouth when I didn't buck the straw off, well, of course, I just let them have their way. Bags of straw on my back with those delicious cubes in my mouth was an easy agreement.

When the day came that my owner slowly climbed on my back it was little different to having the bags of straw. In fact, after a few weeks I began to enjoy these times as I found it reassuring to have someone else making the decisions to avoid stepping on muck forks or buckets left accidentally in the yard. By far the greatest benefit of having someone on my back, a rider, they called it, was that we got to go out of the yard, down country lanes and across fields. Oh, yes, I had been out in the home fields a lot, but these were fields and woods that were new to me. I found I could splash through streams, even go into the sea up to my belly and swim, and, as for speed, well, I could easily outrun my owners, could even escape. But why would I want to do that when I had a secure home with food and a lovely straw bed at night?

I was fast asleep on my snug straw bed one night when my stable door clinked open. This was completely out of my normal routine. Obviously, I jumped up to my feet as I smelled the stench of a different man in the darkness. He approached me and before I could do anything, I felt a sharp stab in my neck. Within just a minute or two I felt all drowsy and wanting to sleep again. I didn't have much recollection of being walked out of the stable, down the yard to the lane outside and into a horse box parked there but, as soon as I was on the straw bed in the box, I collapsed and went fast asleep.

It was a long and satisfying sleep and by the time I awoke to the jolting of the horse box I could see that it was full daylight. I began to realise that, assuming this horsebox had been travelling all night, I must be somewhere miles away. Then I noticed two other ponies that were just waking up in the straw looking as bewildered as I.

I moved over to a small grill on the side of the box where I could look out and I noticed that this must be an incompetent driver as he was driving on the wrong side of the road. Even the road signs were peculiar as they were in a foreign language, not Sussex writing that I was used to. It was a pity that us ponies can't communicate with our neighs as I would have asked them what was happening.

Quite unexpectedly we were all thrust forward as the horse box came to a halt. Gathering our feet, we could hear strange words coming from the people outside, both men's and women's voices. One voice I understood said "Get the ponies out."

Another voice said, "Non, ce poney est calme, cinq cents euros, s'il vous plaît"

I didn't hear the rest but, in a dazed feeling found myself being led into yet another horse box. This next trip was what they called an Autoroute. This was boring, very boring for at least a couple of hours. Judging by the sun we seemed to be heading southwards. After a couple of hours, we pulled into a farmyard and I heard,

"Mettez le poney dans une étable et nous le verrons demain" I didn't have clue what this meant but found myself being dragged out and shoved into a stable. I was not happy with this. No supper. No warm straw bed. I had no intention of staying in this obscene, cruel farm.

These thieves, rustlers they call them that I have since found out, had stolen me from my devoted English family. There was no way I was going to stay in this stable.

After all their lights went out, I investigated my stable. It was pretty basic with just a slide-bolt. So, when all was calm and quiet, I leaned over and used my tongue to slide the bolt open. There were no lights switched on as I walked and then trotted out of this alien yard. I headed for the hill in the distance. I galloped hard and fast to be rid of this hell.

It wasn't so difficult to keep my progression in a northerly direction to aim for my home. The stars did help but I don't think many people realize that us ponies have an innate ability to know in which direction we want to go. I heard people say that Pigeons can do this. Darkness enlightened to dawn and I traversed the many fields growing crops of corn or beans.

One village I arrived at the next day had a market in the market square. Yes, there was a lot of shouting and waving of fists. I left them open-mouthed as I galloped past many stalls selling their produce. Sorry, I grabbed a long length of bread, that had a label, "Baguette" as I passed by the baker's stall.

Still munching the baguette, with no one following, I came across a horse show. All the ponies and horses were tethered to their horse-box owners. So, I had no problem in galloping past their next ring commitments. The loudspeaker shouted, "le propriétaire du poney lâche s'il vous plaît le sécuriser." I guessed this was something to do with me as lots of people tried to stop me. Finally, I arrived at the ship they called, the Channel Ferry. On trotting up the ramp they stopped me as I was not a human with a passport. They said, there was no person leading me. They turned me away and pushed me back down the Ferry ramp.

So, I considered my options. There was a closer port to my destination. That is the port of Rye. It was only 32 miles which I reckon I could swim. Yes, you don't realize how well the water supports my weight and I just keep paddling as if I was doing a slow trot. I found a sandy shore where I could see white cliffs in the distance and trotted into the water from the beach watched by several astounded families sitting on the sand and paddling. The only thing I had to watch out for were these enormous tankers. They all missed me easily and, as planned, I swam up the Rother river into Rye, to Strand Quay, where I found a ramp. By now it was dark, so no one notice me staggering up the ramp onto dry land. I was quite exhausted and even the late passers-by didn't seem to be much concerned as I lay on my side and had a long rest; I fell asleep.

I was up with the dawn as the seagulls shouted their consternation at this intrusion into their usual habitual activity of pinching chips from tourist's fish and chip take-aways. Someone must have reported my slumber on Strand Quay because a police car pulled up by the Strand and the officers looked concerned at my intrusion into their touristy-lawn area. Obviously, I jumped up when I realized that they were about to confront me and galloped swiftly past them onto the main road. They had no chance of getting me as, it was easy to out-run a police car on the Rye roads which are mostly one-way. Yes, I went the wrong way up several roads with cars hooting and putting their brakes on.

Trotting out of Rye town in a westerly direction I was aware of yet another police car shadowing me on the A259. If I didn't stop trotting, they would not be able to stop me so I had this "stand-off" situation where, they wouldn't stop me, and I kept going so as not to disrupt the traffic and cause hold-ups.

It wasn't long before I started to recognize the fields and farms near my lovely owner's farm. In the distance I could see my farm entrance and one final burst of my sapping energy, arrived at our farm and slowed to a walk as I went in. Everyone in the yard heard my hooves on the concrete and stood with amazement and disbelief written across their faces. Then there were lots of shouting and I even had hugs and kisses as my owner threw her arms around my sweaty, still salty, neck.

I was given a heroic reception; yes, carrots, kisses, a wash-down to get the salt off me and the deepest straw bed you could imagine.

The rustlers?

Well, yes, they had they're cum-upance. They were identified by their fingerprints on my stable door. The French authorities have successfully convicted them of rustling theft. They went to prison and I found security, love and freedom.

Do I Like November?

My coat has grown much longer as the daylight fades away.
The grass is not so green or lush; they've started feeding hay.
  The east wind bites and joins the north; a chilling
  two-edged blade,
  to bleach the green in dusty white, a carpet heaven made.

The other day she saddled up, just before the dark.
Scary painted face she had; I knew it was some lark!
  I heard her mention, "Halloween" and off we went with cheer
  but when she knocked on houses just tomatoes hit my rear!

The day I dragged a cart around with sack of straw and face.
"Penny for the guy!" They shout while trotting out apace.
  The smell of baked potatoes and some sausage cooked in fire,
  the reek of beer, the shouts of glee, that extraordinary pyre!

Last night there were explosions with bright flashes so intense
and needlepoints of colour mingled round one flame so dense;
  licking round a human form, black cloak and pointed hat.
  We galloped round our field in fear; why were they cruel
  like that?

The trees have changed to skeletons; the leaves a soft warm bed.
Fungi flourish furtively, thriving off the dead.
  My hooves are sinking deeper now; mud fever; what a pain!
  But sometimes when the frost has been, I walk on top again.

The nights draw in, the lights come out; I see them round
the eaves;
fairy lights and what is that? A tree! My eye deceives!
  If they can put a fir tree in their window all to see…
  then let them make a straw bed in the living room for me.

A Kick in the Dark

Through the meadows with the tallest grass
there strides a lass alone,
heaving at the ragwort roots
without so much a moan.

She's Alice with the fairest hair,
the groom of Colonel Pace.
Agile, nimble, full of fun
with smile upon her face.

The yard is small, the horses few;
the Colonel overbears.
Raining down his orders
on this lonely lass who dares.

Willingly, devotedly,
she sorts out all her chores.
She never ever questions
the rude manner, she abhors.

Her pay is small and bonus none,
her room is checked for dust.
Even on her one day off
she's asked, "Oh, could you just…"

"Sweep out the yard, sort out the tack."
But Alice keeps her mind;
without a flinch and willingly
for Alice is quite blind.

The yard and tack she cannot see
but sense of touch is strong.
She feels the straw and feels the hay
and knows when owt is wrong.

She smells the oil and soap on tack,
she'll hear a snort or bleat.
The pulp from the beet, her taste decides
if fit for horse to eat.

His horse prepared, the Colonel's off
to take his usual ride;
a woodland trot of just one hour,
sedate and dignified.

"Why has the Colonel gone so long?
His horse is not yet fit.
An hour he said and now it's three.
Oh, please avoid the pit."

Too much to bear, she trudges off
in search, in case, in dark.
But darkness deals her bonus cards,
for scents and sounds make mark.

Then near the pit she smells the sweat
and hears the thrashing hooves.
The groaning Colonel crying out,
the squelch of mud and ooze.

Down she clambers to the scene
with little thought for self.
Straining every sense to find
a stand on muddy shelf.

The Colonel's trapped with leg beneath.
She tugs with all her might.
The horse makes move and out he's dragged;
what now the horse's plight?

The Colonel scrambles out the pit;
But the horse is stuck quite fast.
She tries to turn the horse around
She oft has done when cast.

She feels there's only one way now
amidst the thrashing hooves.
She grasps the buckles on the girth
and strains the pins from grooves.

The saddle stays caught upon a root;
the horse rolls down the bank;
knee deep in mire then on its feet,
mud dripping from its flank.

Alas one hoof, one iron shoe
caught Alice on the brow.
Quite still she lies, so motionless
P'raps dead; and so, what now?

As dawn breaks in the hospital
her eyelids sense the light.
Opening wide to see the sun;
Restored again her sight.

To help a horse in darkness,
or whether it be day,
Rewards may not be on this Earth
but come another way.

LOT
7
T. SMITH'S
AUCTION
~ est 1653 ~

A Lot of Horse Sense

"But darling we've hummed and hawed for weeks on this;
  shall we, shan't we, can we, can't we?
It's an opportunity that we shouldn't miss;
  it's our future ahead and our life that will be."

"I know all that but there's thousands at stake.
  Just once a year this auction of stock
when the Gods and events give us chance for a break
  but a pig in a poke would give us a shock."

"My sweetest, a pig would be so easy and cheap;
  just a sty, a small patch, some food; what a boar!
A racehorse that wins will cost hundreds to keep,
  acres of grass, hay, feed, stables and more."

"The catalogue shows that there are just three;
  a young, one-eyed filly that's not a wise bet.
Another a colt, trained on the sands by the sea
  the third, in our budget, is one we should get."

Looking over the three at the sale,
  the filly was small and had a blind eye.
The colt was too heavy as was crossed with a Dale
  The third, a fine colt, they managed to buy.

So back to the stable and pampered with care
    training on gallops; such a promising pace.
His chances of running seemed to be fair,
    muscles built strong and were ready to race.

Then came the day he was entered to run;
    a Grand National race just seemed to make sense.
The young, one-eyed filly just galloped and won
    but our fine colt came last at each fence.

Returning from Aintree, unloaded the colt;
    "Darling reflect, what we want and what's got.
Now you must realise, that we are at fault,
    we should have bought the filly in the other lot."

A Winter's Tail

Rosie prised off her wellingtons using the wooden heel device that Tommy had made a few years earlier. "Horses all fed." She shouted to Tommy who was just washing his hands. "Brrr, cold out there!" continued Rosie, "Are you ready for breakfast?"

This was the general pattern of a morning in the Blake's household and they both sat down to a breakfast that included eggs from their own chickens. As breakfast proceeded towards the toast and coffee Rosie suddenly exclaimed excitedly. "Hey, Tommy, look at this," Rosie pointed at the ad in the Music Weekly magazine from across the breakfast table.

"Well, darling, just read it out; I've got sticky marmalade on my fingers." Tommy dismissed the magazine with a wave of his hand.

"It's from the London Symphony Orchestra and says, 'Vacancy Cellist invited for audition on the 15th February 2.30pm at the Royal Albert Hall. Download application form on the Orchestra's website where full details are provided.'" Rosie rested the magazine on the table, taking a sip of her coffee while looking up at Tommy who had his mouth open with a mouthful of half chewed toast.

"I can't believe it," Tommy gulped and swallowed the mouthful. "That's tomorrow! How on earth did we not see that ad in previous weeks?"

"Well," Rosie glanced at some of the other ads. "This ad is actually quite tucked away, and we could have easily missed it. You've always wanted to be in a prestigious orchestra and now's your chance. It's a fabulous opportunity. Why don't you go for it?"

"If it had been last week there would have been no problem but my cello bow needs a big repair and I can't get the job done by tomorrow; no music shop is open on a Sunday let alone someone specialised in bow repair; such clever folk are like gold dust!" Tommy flopped back in his chair with a look of dejection and despair.

What's wrong with your bow then?" Rosie stood up and started clearing the table.

"Oh, nothing much" he answered sarcastically, "It's just that the bow hairs have worn right through, many strands are actually broken, and I certainly can't take the chance that it will collapse during the audition. Anyway, without a proper hair bow it won't play a recognisable note!"

"Well, darling, I believe that everything in life is possible!" Rosie stopped clearing the table and stood full front to Tommy with her hands on her hips in a defiant posture. "What are those bow-hairs made of?"

"Well, they are made from the tail hairs of a Mongolian stallion. Apparently, stallion tails have just the right structure for producing a clean note on a stringed instrument." Tommy was still looking dejected.

"Come-on, Tommy, darling; think! Just think!" Rosie was now standing just a foot away looking fiercely into Tommy's eyes.

"I am pondering," replied Tommy with a questioning look on his face.

"Have I got to spell it out, my love?" Rosie continued with her concentrated look into Tommy's eyes. "We may not have a Mongolian stallion, but we do have a Highland stallion with a long, wiry tail."

"You don't mean?" Tommy's mouth opened in mid-sentence and continued in a tone of extraordinary realisation. "You mean we could use our stallion tail hair to repair the bow?"

"It's obvious, darling. You don't have any option. Your bow needs new horse hair, and special hair at that, and you have exactly what you need standing out in the stable. I could wash and comb the hair; all you must do is fix it to the bow. Is that easy to do?" Even as she spoke, Rosie was poking around in the kitchen drawer looking for the heavy scissors.

Tommy started to perk up and his mind went into overdrive. "It's a chance, I suppose. I've nothing to lose other than a red face if it doesn't work. Oh, yes, it's straight forward fixing the hair to the bow. At least it will work for the audition and I can get the proper hairs fixed later."

Rosie spent little time finding the scissors, putting on her boots and warm coat and disappearing out into the stable yard to switch on the lights. Titan, the Highland stallion, had never had his tail cut as that was always a feature in the show ring that the judges were keen to see a long, flowing tail; a showing feature of all Highland ponies. He was still eating his breakfast of sugar beet and mix so stood quite still and unconcerned while his tail was cut. On returning to the kitchen Rosie immersed the tail hair into warm soapy water and then did a second wash before a good rinse. Fortunately, the tail hairs had remained in line like an unstranded rope. It didn't take long to dry the strands with her hair dryer during which time Tommy was busy on the computer downloading and filling in the application form.

After the form had been returned by email, Tommy then got an email back saying his application had been received and the auditioning committee were looking forward meeting him the next day. Tommy then spent the next couple of hours selecting hairs that were the right length, not curly and all of a similar colour.

When the fixing was finally done Tommy gave the hairs a generous dose of Rosin, the wax that is always put on the bow hairs in order to get the required tone from the instrument.

"Darling, this is perfect!" exclaimed Tommy as he stroked the bow across the strings. "These hairs seem even better than those Mongolian ones. Why did we never think of this before? We could start a new industry here."

"Oh, no you don't!" replied Rosie, "If you think I'm going to breed lots of stallions for your bow-hair you can think again! It's hard enough having just one stallion to look after.

There were only three cellists at the audition and the three committee judges made a point of mentioning what a lovely romantic tone Tommy had achieved out of his instrument and fortunately they didn't pay much attention to the structure of the bow. The other two cellists were not able to come up to the same standard as Tommy who spent no time in signing the contract. He never let on to anyone in the orchestra when he was introduced on the first evening of rehearsal, but years later wrote the story of the winter's tail!

Garden Capers

There's a pony in my garden and it's grazing on the lawn.
It's ruined the gazebo, which has hoof marks and is torn.
    It's got a hairy mane and tail and eyes that glint with glee;
    how I'm going to catch this colt we will have to see.

He hasn't got a halter and I haven't got a rope.
I grab a tasty carrot and approach with bait in hope.
    He lifts his head and spies the treat but doesn't move an inch.
    Cautiously I take a step; it's got to be a synch!

I hold the carrot out arms length a sniff beneath his nose.
In one swift bite he grabs a half but springs back on his toes,
    swivels round and gallops off with hoof marks making dents,
    makes to jump into the veg demolishing the fence.

Now he's munching at my sprouts with cabbage next in line.
He's obviously starving so now he's eating mine.
    I try again to follow him and get up very near;
    he spins away, kicks both back feet that whistle past my ear.

Have patience, people say to me; they'll give up when worn out.
Talk quietly in whispers but I just want to shout!
    And now it's done a dropping on my flowerbed; that's good,
    fertilize the hyacinths, behaving, as it should.

He spies my little greenhouse with tomatoes snug inside,
casually walks up to it and itches his backside.
  The crash and tinkle frighten him as off he takes again,
  headlong for my swimming pool that I forgot to drain.

In he jumps with bulging eyes straight through the solar sheet;
he must have thought the covering was solid for his feet.
  Blue plastic, water, thrashing hooves all mingled in his fret
  until he finds the Roman steps, he clambers dripping wet.

He's had enough and gallops to the gate he leaps in vault,
rushes through, avoiding cars all screeching to a halt.
  Down the road he slaloms, as cars go squeak and bump
  Pursued by my half carrot as it hits him on his rump.

The Grass Can Be Greener

I stand in mud, my hooves sink deep,
my canter's gone, I only creep.
My bones stick out, my skin has lice,
my water bucket's full of ice.

Will no one come to bring some hay?
Will this be just like yesterday?
With grass all gone, I yearn for food;
I can't remember last I chewed.

With hedges high and padlocks tight,
no one around can see my plight.
Cold and thin, just left to die;
Will no-one even cast an eye?

No saddle will I see again,
no gallop through the tough terrain,
no people sitting on my back,
no smell of oil and soap on tack.

No more rugs to keep me warm,
no more stabling from the storm.
Where is the help from up above?
There's no more strokes, or hugs, or love.

My useful life is gone, they said,
"Her age is wrong, an ugly head."
Why did they make me have a foal?
This sapped my life, my heart and soul.

I feel life ebbing, time is nigh.
I can't shed tears but make a sigh.
The cold bites deep, the hunger throes;
my life now rests with one who knows.

I hear the chink of lock and chain;
the five-barred gate has moved again.
A halter rope is fixed to me;
from this foul field I may be free?

Then I see the rescue truck,
just in time they came with luck.
Now it's fun to be alive
when life begins at twenty five.

It's a Horse's Life

Oh, no, contractions starting now.
My mummy's giving birth to me; does she know just how?
Out I pop into this world with squeeze and push and force;
I can't believe my eyes, good grief! My mummy is a horse!

Oh, no, the grass is cold and damp.
My legs are long; I try to stand despite the pangs of cramp.
My mother licks voraciously; I give another thrust
and up I stand with legs all splayed; the milk bar, what a bust!

Oh, no, the vet is on his way,
with flashy car and student nurse; a routine op' they say.
First of all a sedative, the needle makes me jolt.
I wake up feeling randy but no longer am a colt.

Oh, no, they're putting on the tack.
Time to break me in, they say, with people on my back.
Is it any wonder that I buck and jump around?
It's much more fun, with audience, to put them on the ground.

Oh, no, there's a stallion over there.
Not content with twenty wives he thinks I am a mare.
A massive leap, he clears the hedge but doesn't see the pool;
splashing in up to his neck, his ardour now quite cool.

Oh, no, it's market time today.
Load me on a cattle truck, lot 62, they say.
In the ring he leads me round and prods me with a stick.
I smile awhile, to claps and cheers, as in his groin I kick!

Oh, no, it's summertime again.
The bot fly's here, the horse fly's rife and midges are a pain.
The hay is cut, the grass is lush; I'm munching all I can.
I also sunbathe in the nude but never get a tan!

Oh, no, they're going to a show
Plaiting up my mane and tail, brushing to and fro.
I love to jump the fence and poles and when I feel inclined
I fly-buck in the air so hard my rider stays behind.

Oh, no, they've put a novice on my back.
Hired me out for money to a fat man for a hack.
Is it any wonder that when we turn for home
I buck him in the gutter and gallop back alone.

Oh, no, it's time for snow and ice;
mud fever on my leggy bits and body full of lice.
Digging out New Zealand rugs to keep me snug and warm
only to find the rats came first with holes all tat and torn.

Oh, no, I can't believe my eyes;
they're dressing up in fancy dress and putting on disguise.
And now they've hitched me to a sledge, and made my nose all red. Why have they made me look like that with antlers on my head?

Robin

I'm Robin, quite a heavy horse and kind as you could find.
My life is full of wonder even though my eyes are blind.
I lost my sight when I was young, I fell and hit my head;
better to survive and live, rather than be dead.

A horse cannot have a guide dog; I must find a way
to find my food and water, graze the fields and even play.
Yes, play is fun for ponies too, horses, mules and so
we live a life, as humans do, enjoying life, you know.

Fortunately, a stable hand will often lead me round
and puts the hay and water where I've learnt that it be found.
My other senses are acute; I hear and smell, so now
every nook and cranny, knowing where and what and how.

There are those days when we tack up to ride out for a hack.
Bridle, saddle, girth just right, she mounts up on my back.
She knows I'm blind and will take care; my safety is to be;
we even make a gallop when the way ahead is free.

I remember when, one sunny day, we were riding out
along the beach and on the sand, my rider gave a shout,
"Beware there, my horse can't see!" to bathers makes a call.
They jump up, grab their towels while shouting insults all.

My rider shouts out, “Sorry,” as we leave the angry throng.
I had a horsey feeling that we’d been and done some wrong.
Some letters to the Council spoke of danger on the sand
and ‘stop the riding on the beach’ and ‘rule it out of hand’.

Another sunny morning when my owner said, “prepare
to raise some funds for blind folk at the local village fair.”
Lots of fun, the razzmatazz, the noise and kids at play;
carrots, pats, strokes and smells, enjoyments of the day.

Oh, here we go with pony rides, they ignore that I’m a horse;
well you can’t expect the public to distinguish me, of course!
So, up and down, round and round, I walk up with a child
and even have one large, fat man that makes my back defiled.

When all the pony rides are done, I munch some hay and grass.
I notice that I’m all alone; why let this moment pass?
Now’s my chance to make escape and freedom from a rope.
I tug and break and seize my chance for freedom fuelled
with hope.

Off I gallop round the fair, their faces all in shock.
They can’t believe a horse so big is free to run amok.
The flower tent is my first choice, its floral scent is near.
First prize goes to Dahlias, my hooves have squashed, oh dear!

Then I smell the rabbit tent with cavies, rats and mice.
All cages knocked wide open, just a kick I find, suffice.
Freedom for those rodent folks, they jump and run in joy,
with lady stewards on the chairs with dresses up all coy.

I hear lots of bees a-buzzing in the bee-tent just nearby.
I gallop over tables stacked with honey jars to buy.
The broken hives of honeybees lets swarms of bees to rout;
sticky honey, angry bees; me and all run out.

Then I smell the food tent where the women sell their goods;
Cornish pasties, cakes and rolls, some pies and summer puds.
Here I take a gentle stroll while nibbling here and there.
Now having had my fill with food I leave without a care.

The dog show ring has bunting round, I hear those doggies bark.
The bunting catches round my chest; well this can be a lark!
Doggies chasing bunting breaking free and off they run;
their owners shouting after them, but dogs are having fun.

The brass band plays a different tune as mayhem renders through.
The trumpeter jumps out the way; the tuber man turns blue.
The cornet player dives beneath the slide-tromboner's chair;
the kettle drummer beats retreat; conductors going spare.

Then there's tea with jam and cake, the women's Institute.
Their tent is always heaving with their pasties, pies and fruit.
They're all so passive sitting there, while knitting, as you know,
but in I gallop, dogs in chase, wreaking havoc as we go.

Tables knocked, fruit gets squashed, the doggies have a feast.
An apple pie falls on my head but that's not even least.
Two dogs get tangled in the pins and strands of knitting wool
while others eat the porky pies, and all become quite full.

They throw some doughnuts after us as onwards we run free.
Where next the stalls or tents that we can run while on our spree?
But then I hear a siren as a police car stops near me.
That makes me trot, then walk and stop; they tie me to a tree.

My owner catches up with me and loads me in the box.
She says I've been quite naughty but that's a paradox.
Excitement in the fair they want, and I gave them all just that.
Life becomes so boring; I just turn up the thermostat!

I shouldn't let it end here with me saying I did well.
There're many blinded animals that live through living hell.
Just take a moment in your thoughts and all your working strife,
only you, a human being, has the skill to give us life.

"I, Tommy, Resolve…"

…To eat up the hay in manger but never when there's dust;
to drink my water quietly but not if there's any rust;
to chew my carrots properly, not swallow when they're whole
or make my rug all muddy when I lay down for a roll.

…Try not to nip the fingers of the hand with sugar lump;
and not to kick the farrier when he tickles on my rump;
not to kick the door in when it's feeding time again
or scratch my neck on barbed wire that pulls out all my mane.

…Not to stamp my bucket when the water's all been drunk;
not to neigh and whinny when the stable door goes clunk.
Never tease that barking dog that tries to nip my heals,
or stand and gloat as I kick hard and off it runs and squeals!

…When she tightens up my girth, I mustn't bloat with air
and keep my mouth quite open when the bit is pushed in there.
When my rider starts to mount, I always stand quite still
and when she loses both the irons, not gallop down the hill.

…To travel to the horse show with my tail still plait and clean
    and not to chat up fillies in the ring next door I've seen.
To always make the judge aware that I am handsome too,
not embarrass judge and owner such as going to the loo.

    …To eat up all my vegetables to keep the vet bills low
    and keep myself quite fit and trim and ready for a show.
So, when it's time to go for rides we make a jolly pair,
in harmony, togetherness; she'll know I really care.

Greek Lament

If your lot in this world be a donkey in Greece
    you will live in the chasm of hell,
with the load on my back giving little release
    from the pain of my skeletal shell.

Why do they expect that I carry such weight,
    I give them my life, what it's worth?
I buckle, deform, collapse and frustrate
    to the pain of that severing girth.

The lice are so rife gorging blood from my veins;
    no medical care for a mute.
In agony, itching and rubbing my pains
    while whipped by a muleteer brute.

Bald patches of skin; that festering sore;
    no rest from the flies and the heat.
They drink up my tears, eyes chafe to their core
    and cars bang my legs in the street.

…now time has taken its toll…

Unable to work, abandoned and lost,
    compassion has found my retreat.
To England I go; what rescue, what cost?
    A heaven, my life now complete.

Last Ride of the Knight

The rush of the wind as headlong we flee,
the breathing, the gasping, entangled in speed;
saliva of beast in froth flinging free,
confetti in praise of this super steed.

The drumming of hooves, the pounding of steel,
flinging the earth snow-black in the sky.
The leather in urgency groaning surreal;
the clink of the scabbard on irons and the thigh.

The smells of the ditches, the flowers, the pine;
the stench of the sweat all lathered in hair
mingled with oil in tack on the spine;
the breath from the lungs consuming the air.

No trot in the park, no canter in fun,
this mare has control in the gallop she moves.
They chase for my life; my fate could be won.
I cradle my heart in the thrashing of hooves.

The mail weighs so heavy, the helmet feels dank;
the spear is now lost, the sword is in hand.
Galloping, urging, spurring the flank;
the shoes make a churning and chopping the land.

Do they come near me? Are they behind?
        What arrow deserves me? What spear in my back?
Will they be faster? What haste will they find?
        I pray to my maker for all that I lack.

Chasing the brow of the hill, now she's weary,
        reaching the height to reveal all below.
There be pavilions with standards so cheery
        seeming to beckon with folds to bestow.

Keep on, my sweet charger, my spurs are no more.
        My wound makes me fainter so here I must fall.
Your groom 'waits you yonder with oats held in store.
        Farewell my fine pure-bred, you gave me your all.

No, Mate!

All through the summer days Jane kept lean and fit,
    trotting round the meadows, cantering out on moors.
Gallops through the local woods and champing on her bit;
    even in her stable she never kicked the doors.

But as the summer sun declined and Autumn leaves
were browned
    Janey started eating well so feed and oats cost dear.
Gone went her slim form, out bulged her tummy mound,
    yet never had a stallion been anywhere so near.

Was on one winter's eve that Janey's foal came late;
    a lanky, legged filly with a white star 'tween her ears.
This is now a mystery? She never had a mate.
    Seems even in the equine world virgin birth appears.

A Pony Christmas Present

Holly sprigs with dates and figs;
Ivy walls and cold, bleak stalls,
chilled on concrete, ice in hooves,
endure the squalor, boss reproves.
So, where's the love she said I'd live?
Where's the rug that she could give?
There's sadness in my heart at Christmas,
even though she says I'm precious.
Roll on Spring; new owner bring!

Just right now I wonder how
and what's the reason carol season?
Swig the wine and stuff the turkey,
ignore my stable damp and murky.
Light the pudding, cut the cake;
my straw bed, no time to make.
Emotions lapse, my spirit saps;
no longer feel, my hurt won't heal.

Forget me, yes; you wouldn't guess,
we also make, for pony's sake
a Christmas party, our decision,
never seen by human vision.
Lots of neighing, stamping, weaving,
even flirting, get my meaning?
Next year's goal, I raise my foal!
My best pressy; love to all!

My Eyes are Yours

Just a few more steps so follow me close;
  the water is near,
  the ripples are clear.
No need to be anxious, sad or morose;
  I love you, my dear.

Blind as you are as the depths of the night;
  companion of old,
  your sight has been sold
by the thorns in the hunt of the fox in full flight.
  My love is untold.

Keep your nose to my flank for the field is quite vast.
  My eyes are but yours;
  I live for this cause.
Listen my snorts and mimic what's past;
  love cannot pause.

No rest for my eyes as I see for your frame,
  alert for your fears,
  while humans shed tears.
Be thankful you're equine, not 'ritic or lame;
  our love grows in years.

And so, to the trough and I slurp so you sense.
    Tingle the trough
    or try to make cough:
my noise to your ears are your eyes feeling whence
    is my love; is enough?

And so, I am thrilled at the gulp of your drink
    as you relish the burst
    of your quenching the thirst,
fusing our love, our wonderful link;
    our love that comes first.

Oh, hell to the punters and hunters in haste;
    the thorns took your sight
    in the fury of flight;
to squander your eyes for a thrill; what a waste!
    My love is your light.

The Day of the Knight

Bending on the halyard to that sheet-white bunting
splayed across the middle with those deep, red lines.
    Hauled to the truck
    of the slim, white spruce pole,
Proud to show off England with St George's shrines.

Martyrdom in Palestine, patron Saint of England,
burnished in his armour 'stride this great, white steed,
    seeking that cavern
    where lies the monster.
He's fearless in adversity and dangers never heed.

My hooves were digging deeper as I carried his burden,
confident my master would be righting that was wrong.
    Maidens under bondage;
    Princess was a hostage.
Death forebodes that creature with the fiery tongue.

Reigning on my snaffle-bit we neared the cave entrance;
shouted to the scaly brute to heed our call.
    With a thundering roar,
    teeth gleaming and claw,
his tail smacks my pastern bone that makes me fall.

George had held his seating but my flaxen mane is burning.
I pushed with all my equine might to take my stand.
    Finding the chink,
    where the spike could sink,
and the lance just drove deeper by the thrust of George's hand.

Never do forget our roots, our fabled myths and legends.
Hoist the flag of passion on St Georges Day.
    Twenty third of April,
    England ever grateful
to the horse that bore the victor to the dragon that was slay.

Saying Goodbye

You're a person, supposedly a human, with compassion
in your veins;
    and yet you keep this stallion confined in dark and chains.
The stable's just a prison where the steed is innocent
    Just to suit your selfish whims, your egocentric bent.

Fortunately, I came one night, I cropped the lock and wire.
    Yes, I stole that super steed, that magnificent Shire.
I tied the sacks around his hooves to deaden any sound;
    so willingly he strided out, so softly on the ground.

A moment's hesitation as he wondered at the box,
    the darkness just revealing fetching, leg-white socks.
Then up he strides in freedom and the ramp is closed and tight,
    I drive off very gently with the life I saved that night.

The sun was just a peeping as the dawn awoke to break
    A long drive, a steady drive, for the horse's sake.
Into the yard I turned the box relieved the deed was done.
From prison filth and starving to his freedom earned and won.

Not a dungeon for you, Shire, you're free now for a roam,
a lush grass field all to yourself that you can call your own.
Gallop free, enjoy the breeze and stretch your heart's desire;
no more darkness, no more whips, you're free you great entire!

No police have come a-knocking, and the neighbours
couldn't care.
Deep grass, the sunlight's free and even has a mare
The vet has come to check his state and see that all is well.
Stethoscope and samples; later, back he rings to tell.

Confinement in the darkness, the stress, the lice, the worm
have done severe and lasting damage to his organs for
long term.
"I'm sorry that it's terminal; he cannot live for long."
The vet is full of sympathy and I wonder if he's wrong?

Of course, he's not; the facts are clear, the animal is quite ill.
His eyes look into mine to plead his life, his soul, my will.
Goodbye my brave, big Shire; all my love I give and… bang!
Majestically he crumbles as the pistol echo rang.

A Ride in Spirit

So, you're my rider for today
dressed in tweeds with money to pay.
    Fresh from the town with whip-slapping thigh,
    pretending your knowledge is vast; it's a lie.

Your floozy rides well but you are a sham.
You're so overweight by many a gram.
    You last rode a donkey down on the sands
    and now I have to put up with your hands.

My groom fits my saddle well on my back
with bridle all snug, I'm ready for hack.
    Your foot in the stirrup and rise to the seat
    I bet you're so chuffed you managed this feat.

Now you're so close my nostrils do flare;
you smell of cheap brandy, so what do I care?
    Drunk in charge of a galloping steed;
    Your life is in danger, be sober, take heed.

No one has noticed that you cannot ride.
You told them you could, but I know you lied.
    There are all sorts of reasons to stop and dismount
    but, no, you keep on, your money must count.

Your spurs in my belly are making me heed.
Your hands at the reins on the bit make me bleed.
Why rein me in while spurring to go?
Like the brake and the gas on a car, don't you know?

You're pounding my back and hurting my spine;
you can't even keep me in a straight line.
Why whip me in anger, I carry your weight?
This ride reads disaster, I despair of our fate.

Galloping over the fields and the meadows
into the gloom of the woods and the shadows;
missing the oaks and brushing the pine,
your life on my back has outgrown its time.

There be a ditch you think I will jump.
Your spurs dig me deep and hurt to my rump.
Closer and closer and now it seems deep;
dare, even I, to give such a leap?

There's no going back as over we go.
The mud is so soft, the jump is so slow.
My hooves, in the frenzy, have missed the far bank.
I panic and clamber but down it I sank.

My ears hear the crack as my spine breaks its bone.
Fate has decided that I die here alone.
My rider survives to booze yet again.
How many more great steeds will be slain?

The Lost Pony – a children's story

Susan was walking back from school across the fields when she came upon a skewbald pony.

"What is your name, little pony?" asked Susan.

"My name is Jimmy," answered the pony, "and I am lost. The horrible man that was riding me fell off and I galloped away. Can you help me find my stable?"

Susan patted the pony and replied, "Of course I will; I know where you live. Shall I ride on your back or lead you by your reins?"

"Oh, ride on my back, please," replied the Jimmy.

Susan mounted Jimmy's back and sat comfortably on the saddle. "Walk on, Jimmy" urged Susan with a little squeeze of her legs. "You belong to Farmer Giles who lives near my house."

Jimmy and Susan walked across the field and through a gate where they met a cow.

"Hello cow! What is your name and what are you doing here?"

"My name is Daisy and I am lost. I was frightened when a dog chased me out of my field. Can you show me the way back, please?"

"Follow us," replied Susan. "I know your field as you belong to Farmer Giles, which is where we are going."

"OK," replied Daisy and she followed behind Jimmy as he walked on.

Then they came to a cat sitting in the field with big tears rolling down its sad, furry face.

"Why are you sitting in the field crying?" asked Susan to the cat.

"I was chasing a mouse and it ran out of the farmyard," replied the cat. "Now I am lost. Can you help me find my home?"

"Yes, of course we can," answered Susan. "Climb on Daisy's back; we are going to Farmer Giles' farmyard where you live.

Felix, the cat climbed on Daisy's back and they all set off across the fields.

Soon they came to a little mouse sitting in the field and when he saw them, he scurried away. Immediately, Felix the cat, jumped off Daisy's back and chased after the mouse. Daisy then decided to chase after the cat. Jimmy and Susan trotted behind Daisy.

The mouse ran into Farmer Giles' farmyard where it ran down a hole. Then everyone stopped still.

"Look everyone," said the surprised Daisy. "We are back at our home!"

"Yes," smiled Susan. "You didn't really need me as the clever, little mouse showed us the way."

Making Jumpers

You're greedy, you breeder, you bred me for racing,
hiding behind the glamour on course.
Pitching my skills to the fences I'm facing,
making me jump with a whip to enforce.

At two years of life came the saddle I heed.
I'm stabled and groomed for the make.
Your greed for my speed dishonours my breed;
cannons bred lighter and break.

Our noses are born to filter the dust
keeping dirt to our lungs under check.
I'm breathing just right, but money you lust,
gash a hole to my throat in the neck.

Pain-masking drugs like bute from the pack
does little to mend all my ills.
You don't give a damn! You keep me on track;
your odds on the day are what kills.

Under vet's knife, your surgery's flawed,
my tendons and muscles are cursed,
as, later in life, when I'm not insured,
the pain being lame is much worse.

The Chair and the Beeches have taken their toll
    and many a fence has seen death.
Breeders close ranks as there's punters involved;
    make money from out my last breath.

The Equine Writer

There must be some cardboard spread across the floor
for me to write a letter or a word or two or more.
Awkward shapes are numbers, those from two to ten,
as I'm a horse with shiny hooves that cannot hold a pen.

I write the letter "I" quite well with black paint on my hoof.
My master says it is a word with dictionary proof.
I also write a great big "E" but that gets me in a tangle
I must make a turn left for three strokes at right angle.

Words with curves I can't abide, like 'super', 'moaner', 'rue'.
But all the words with straight bits are a synch for me to do,
especially when they're capitals, with words like 'TILL'
and 'TANNIN',
or leaving off the 'G' from 'ING', like 'EATIN', 'DATIN'
or 'FAINTIN'.

"Just a horse," you may say, "of course he cannot write.
His front legs only do one stroke; the line is black but right."
Yes, straight lines are my forte, I cannot make those curves.
That's where my master links with me in writing, voice
and nerves.

He measures all my thoughts so well and turns them into words;
sentences with adjectives, participles and verbs;
phrases with conjunctions, adverbs, nouns, I've seen.
He doesn't even use a pen, just board, a box, and screen.

If I stroll around a field to graze or stand and dose
he comes out with his camera and tries to make me pose.
That saddle is another thing he straps onto my back;
adorned with bitted bridle, we trot out for our hack.

Hacking down the country lanes or hunting with the Meets
always seems to make him tired but after, feeds me treats.
Then such words come pouring out and often in a rhyme;
keyboard tapping, flickering screen accounting of our time.

I call myself a writer through my master and his pen.
A horse with brains and hoof can forge a link with any men.
Inspire yourself with any pet, their antics and their foods;
just write about our lives, our loves, our habits and our moods.

A Cheap Farrier?

Having found local farriers on Google, Vicky dialled one that wasn't too far away.

"Hello, is that Mr. Dixon, the farrier?"

"Yes, lass, that's me."

"Oh, Mr Dixon, I've rung several other farriers about shoeing my pony, but they all charge such enormous fees of over £50."

"Oh, yes!"

"Yes, Mr. Dixon, and what is more they all add on extra for travelling."

"Oh, yes."

"Well, Mr. Dixon, I wondered if your charge is more realistic, me being a student, and it's only a pony?"

"Well, er, yes, I could be more realistic. I tell you what, I'll not make any charge for transport. How's that?"

"Oh, Mr. Dixon, you're the first one to knock off the travelling charge. When can you come? I'm at Jones' Livery Yard."

"Yes, I know that yard. Well, I guess I can come straight away after I finish this job I'm doing. Be about an hour."

"That's great. Thank you. I'll be waiting at the yard with my pony, 'Tripsy'. See you then."

"Yup, OK, see you soon."

An hour later…

"Hello, lass, is this your pony, Tripsy?"

"Yes, hello, Mr Dixon, this is Tripsy. You never did say on the phone what your charge was?"

"Well, let me see, it's got to be reasonable for the work I put in. There are four shoes and each shoe will have seven nails. I tell you what, I'll charge you just for the nails. We'll make the first nail one penny, and just double up on that for each nail."

"Oh, you mean the second nail will be two pence, and the third just four pence?"

"Yes, that's right, lass; it won't take long either as he seems a quiet pony."

"Oh, Mr Dixon, that sounds very reasonable and not charging for transport. When you've finished, I shall tell all those other farriers what I think of their exorbitant charges."

The Journey

Just a few more steps to the building site,
bruising, suffering back and the thighs.
If only they would make bricks light.
If only they could hear my cries.

Forty years I've trudged these tracks,
underfed and whipped each day,
just to build these concrete stacks;
curse the firing of bricks from clay.

The years of my life I'm forced to give;
just an animal is what they say
but don't we both have the right to live
respectful of each in our own way.

But now I collapse, my brick load found
too heavy for me; unable to stand.
The shouts I hear as the bricks fall down;
a beating again by my owner's hard hand.

With the heavy load gone I get to my feet
and manage to trot away from the site.
The sun blazes down, I'm weakened by heat;
a future with freedom is surely my right.

At last I find some grass by the side;
they never did feed me any fresh herb.
But then a car pulls up by my hide,
all white and blue and stopped by my kerb.

Police with shears cutting chains from my hocks,
then I see he's making a call.
Later this lady pulls up in a box,
helping me in so I do not fall.

A cosy straw bed I have for the night;
sleep as I've never accustomed before.
A breakfast of carrots, some hay; what a sight!
And a field full of grass, I cannot want more.

There's talk of a journey, a voyage that I hear
with phone calls, letters, passports and more.
Then one day a horsebox draws very near
and us twenty donkeys are loaded on straw.

What a trip we enjoy with plenty of food;
the box on the ship in Biscay was fun.
Rocking and rolling we got in the mood
The weather got colder away from the sun.

Arriving at Ashford, the ramp opened wide
and out we all spewed to a public that gazed.
The next box trip was a two-hour ride
to arrive at our home for the rest of our days.

From the trauma of hell to pastures so green,
from abusive builders in far off Crete,
to a land of compassion where love rules supreme;
such a journey to heaven will never be beat.

The Summer of 1790

The Kings Head Inn by Aldgate stagecoach stop was the favourite for drenching Dick and Jim's thirst after the work with the horses. They had both worked for three years indentured to the well-respected apothecary, Mr John Bligh, who had set up the business several years ago.

"And another thing, Jim, have you noticed lots of foreigners around? French, I guess as they're trying to get away from that revolution going on in France; disgusting how they're cutting off the heads of those they don't want."

"Aye," replied Jim as he called the young wench over for another couple of pints and gave her two half pennies when they arrived a minute later.

"Jim, I heard that our boss's brother has landed at Greenwich. Did you know that?"

"Oh, you mean his brother, William Bligh, the captain of that ship, the Bounty. Yes, his crew mutinied and put him in a boat with some of his loyal crew. That's amazing that he managed to get back. I don't think the Navy will let that go; they don't stand for mutiny. I reckon they will send navy ships out to track down the mutineers and string them up. What was that chaps name, Fletcher something?" Jim took a swig of beer from his full tankard.

"Christian," grunted Dick. "Name was Christian. Now that's not a very Christian thing to do with a name like that. Yes, Fletcher Christian, that's his name. Shouldn't have a name like that if you're doing a dastardly deed."

"Aye, they're gonna have a job to find that guy as he sailed off. He could be anywhere now." Jim settled his tankard onto the rustic wooden table, placed both hands astride on the table and stood up. "Time for the sack, Dick. It's an early start again tomorrow to cut that colt that Bligh suspects might be a rig."

"Yes, Jim, there's normally a hansom cab outside this time of night; do you want to share it again? You know how Harriet likes you to arrive in a cab to impress the neighbours."

The cab was waiting there with the horse munching from the nose-bag which was dangling down from around his ears.

"Carton Close, Poplar, please cabby," Dick called as they both climbed into the back, and, after removing the nosebag and placing it down by his feet, the cabby only had to click his tongue and the horse trotted off.

Dick was awoken next morning, as usual, by his landlady Harriet, and immediately he banged on the wall to awaken Jim next door. Following a quick rinse in the bowl of water and, dressing in their work clothes, the pair arrived downstairs within minutes of each other and tucked into their bread and dripping and a boiled egg.

As he wiped his plate clean Dick asked, "What's the time Harriet?"

"Says quarter to eight, isn't that the time you have to go?"

"Yup, that's it, Harriet. Come on, Dick, we don't want to get old Bligh into a bad mood at the start of the day."

Arriving at the converted stable yard, Jim and Dick were pleased to have arrived before Mr Bligh and immediately set about washing all the instruments that they knew were to be used for the colt's operation. Five minutes later Mr Bligh arrived, dismounted and immediately set about washing his hands, preparing the drugs and starting the colt's operation which went smoothly as the colt was not a rig.

As they were reviving the horse a cab appeared and pulled up to a halt. The smartly dressed gentleman stepped down with a big smile and, looking straight at Mr Bligh and blurted in a loud voice, "John, John Bligh, when was the last time we met?"

Immediately John recognised his brother William and exclaimed, "Bill!" as he ran forward discarding the towel and embracing with arms around each other. "Bill, I won't ask you where you've been as it's been all over the news sheets. How are you? Where are you staying? Have you another ship?"

"Woah, there, one at a time, John." answered William Bligh. "Just a family get-together if you can put me up for a few days?"

"No problem, Bill, of course you can come and stay and stay as long as you like." Then turning to his two apprentices, said, "OK, the gelding has come round. Get it back into the stable and clear up."

Then William remarked, "Before we do anything, John, I need your advice."

"Yes, anything. Go ahead," said John as he started to heat some water for tea.

"Well, you know all this action that is going on in France?" William paused. "Well, seems the revolutionaries need money to effect their campaign."

"Yes, I can understand that may be so." John started to get a couple of tankards from the cupboard.

"Well, seems these revolutionaries are selling any valuables from the rich to whoever will buy, and our Government is one of the buyers. They've even ransacked the royal palace and are selling all the King's valuables, including his horses. It's the horses I am concerned with as our government have purchased seven of King

Louis' horses which arrived at Greenwich yesterday. Furthermore, to get things moving our Government have rewarded me, because of the Bounty experience, with giving me King Louis' personal horse, a magnificent white gelding."

John stopped his tea-making, hovering with amazement. "Wow, Bill, what a present! That horse must be one of the best in the whole of France. You're so lucky."

"Well, John, yes and no. I'm a sailing man, not a horse man. I want you to give it the once over so I can decide whether to keep it or sell it." William looked towards the empty tankards as if expecting the tea.

"Oh, sorry, Bill, I was miles away thinking of that French palace and the horses." John started to make the tea again, continuing, "I can't leave here now and I realise you need advice as soon as possible. I tell you what. One of my apprentices is nearly qualified and I would respect his opinion; he has a lifetime experience of horses and their fitness as well as a good knowledge of their illnesses."

"Whatever you say, John." William accepted the tea. "Thank you. I've written down the address where the horse is now stabled." He passed the note to John who walked straight to the yard and called to Dick.

Confronting Dick and looking sternly into his eyes he said, "Dick, I want you to do me and my brother a favour. Take a cab, here's the money, and go straight to this address where you will see the white gelding purchased from the King of France; it's been donated as a present to Bill. It's only just arrived from across the Channel to Greenwich. I want you to check the horse out in every way and come back with an opinion as to rideability, health, attitude and value. Any questions?"

"No, Mr Bligh. You can rest assured that you will have an honest appraisal of everything about the horse." Dick turned, went into the shed and packed several tools and necessary items into a bag. He then stood in the road to catch the first cabby passing.

Arriving at the stables in Greenwich, Dick introduced himself to the groom, a youngish chap who was clearly in a panic.

Dick explained, "I've been sent by Mr Bligh to see his white gelding and…" before Dick could finish his sentence the groom grabbed his arm and dragged him towards the stable muttering as they went. Dick managed to grasp a few key words, "Gelding ill, rolling, agony," Even before he saw the horse rolling on the ground Dick suspected the worst; and spoke to the groom in a slow, steady voice, "This horse has either a twisted or blocked gut. I must operate immediately. You'll have to be my assistant."

Dick immediately prepared and injected a sedative into the writhing horse's neck and had the groom administering ether near the horse's nose. When the horse was quiet and unconscious Dick set about the operation to expose the obvious part of the intestine, where, sure enough, there was a bulge indicating a blockage.

"This is the problem," Dick pointed out the bulge to the groom. I'm going to slice along that part and remove the obstruction."

The groom nodded and watched as Dick sliced through the bulge which immediately burst out its contents. Dick was expecting a ball of chewed grass but instead there seemed to be two small linen bags tied at the bags' necks. Dick pushed them aside and stitched up the incision followed by more stitching to the horse's belly with a liberal dose of Mr Blyth's secret antiseptic liquid formula.

"OK," sighed Dick, and turning to the groom remarked, "I don't even know your name but thanks for your help and you can stop dripping that ether now. You can see that the blockage culprit was this small bundle of linen. I'll take it back to Captain Bligh and let him see it to prove there was a blockage."

On returning to John Bligh's premises that evening Dick found the brothers were sitting, drinking beer and swapping anecdotes of happenings over the last few years. As Dick entered, Captain Bligh stood up, moved forward and shook Dick's hand.

"Well done lad, I can see you're quite exhausted travelling over there and checking my horse out. So, what do you think?" Captain Bligh stood back and folded his arms expectantly.

Dick took the two linen bags from his pocket and held them towards the Captain, saying, "I'm sorry, Captain, I had to operate on your horse as soon as I got there as it was writhing in agony with a blocked intestine. These two bags were the blockage which I removed. I thought it best that you open the bags; they feel hard and bumpy to me."

"Good Lord, lad, is the horse all right?" Captain Bligh took the two bags as John Bligh now also stood up to see them.

"Oh, yes sir, the horse recovered from the operation well and will be fine but I got to thinking about when the horse would have swallowed these bags probably forcefully as a horse wouldn't swallow them willingly."

As Captain Bligh reached for a knife to cut the strings on the bags, his brother John asked,

"OK, Dick, what is your theory?"

At this point Captain Bligh emptied the contents of both bags onto the table and all were wide-eyed as an array of fine jewels spread across the table in a variety of bright colours.

Dick, also amazed at what he saw, went on, "Well, sir, this was the personal horse belonging to King Louis XVI, and he knew his palace was about to be ransacked. At that time, he probably considered that they would take all his precious possessions, so he had to find a fool-proof way of hiding his more valued jewellery. He had to think up a place where the rioters would not consider looking, so, he put them in these bags, tied up with string and made the horse swallow them, thinking that, after the revolution he would be allowed to have his life and the horse back. I think the revolutionaries were desperate for money and fixed a deal with our Government to buy the horses and by transporting them across the Channel quickly they would also get their money also quickly."

The two brothers Bligh rotated their stare with gaping jaw from the jewels to Dick, and back again and then looked at each other in disbelief.

"Gawd damnit, Dick," said Captain Bligh, "not only can you carry out complex operations but you are also a genius of deduction. Now look here, you two, no one must ever hear of this. John, these were originally King Louis' jewels, but I reckon they are yours now by government gift. I think it would be fair to distribute their value between the three of us, especially young Dick here who did the operation and found them. Well, the horse might have died without the operation and then the bags would have been buried with the horse, never to be found."

The three agreed and subsequently Dick was released from his indentures and became John Bligh's Partner. The horse? Well, Captain William Bligh kept the French, crown's horse and no one ever let on about the jewels discovered inside it.

Acknowledgements

The 21 pen and ink illustrations have been drawn by artist, Verity Brown but each is the result of several sketches that capture a key moment in the narrative.

I searched over the internet for several months to find an artist that could capture the style I wanted and Verity achieved even more than anticipated, so thank you Verity.

Also, I thank my wife, Dinty, for her patience when I was writing and failed to answer her question or summons for a meal. A response with a 'grunt' was not the proper reply from a husband.

- Tony Smith -

About the Author

Tony attended the Royal Hospital School in Suffolk but from the age of 21 has been closely associated with horses. In 1972 he founded the Brownbread Horse Rescue Centre in East Sussex, and both he, and his wife Dinty, run the 50-acre centre. Tony's main career, as a biology specialist, has been in teaching secondary science and the whole spectrum of subjects in primary schools. He was also Head teacher in a special needs school.

His secondary career was in both the Merchant Navy, as Second Mate, and the Royal Fleet Auxiliary, as second officer, where he ended his sea time returning from the Yugoslavian conflict on the ship, 'Fort Grange'. He has taught navigation and seamanship to the Yachtmasters standard and the sea remains very much in his blood; he can, with a fair wind, be spotted sailing his ketch out of Rye and Eastbourne.

In 2007 he was runner-up for the best short story for the National Association of Writers' Groups.

Tony's daughter, Donna, a teacher, and her husband, David, an art director, have a son and twin girls, and Tony's son, Reuben, works in Sahaja, a mountainous retreat in Portugal, with the world-renowned oracle, Mooji.

Available worldwide from Amazon

---

www.mtp.agency

www.facebook.com/mtp.agency

@mtp_agency

Michael Terence Publishing

Made in the USA
Columbia, SC
13 October 2021

46928284R00091